To

From

GRATEFUL
for You

THOMAS NELSON
Since 1798

NASHVILLE   MEXICO CITY   RIO DE JANEIRO

Published in Nashville, Tennessee, by Thomas Nelson.

Cover design by Kathy Mitchell.

Thank you to Steffany Woolsey for her assistance with compiling this book.

Thomas Nelson titles may be purchased in bulk for educational, business, fund-raising, or sales promotional use. For information, please e-mail SpecialMarkets@ThomasNelson.com.

ISBN 13: 978-0-529-12186-8

Printed in China

14 15 16 17 DSC 5 4 3 2 1

www.thomasnelson.com

I'm grateful for you . . .

When I think of
people who have made a
difference in my life,

YOU

quickly come
to mind.

THE TIME
YOU'VE GIVEN,
THE WISDOM
YOU'VE
SHARED . . . . HAS
BLESSED ME.

Perfume and incense
bring joy to the heart,
and the pleasantness
of a friend springs from
their heartfelt advice.

—PROVERBS 27:9

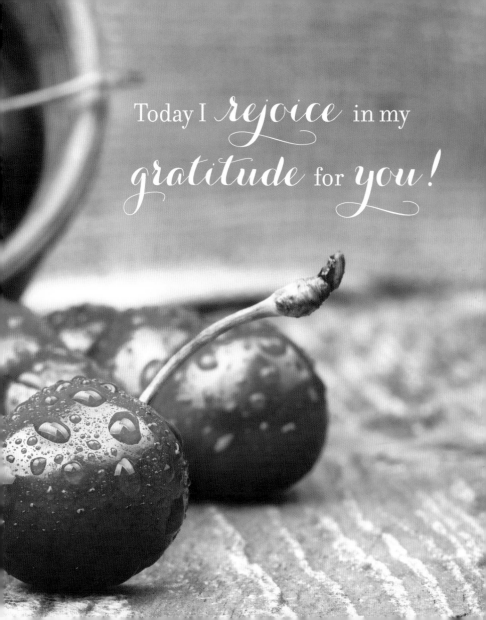

Today I *rejoice* in my *gratitude* for *you!*

When you have been
through hard times and
come out the other side,
look around you.
The people still there are
your true friends.

I'm *thankful*

you have been there for me.

there is

always,

always,

always

something to be thankful for . . .

. . . *you* are one of them

*This is the day that the LORD has made;
let us rejoice and be glad in it.*

PSALM 118:24 ESV

EVERY NOW AND
THEN, IT'S GOOD TO
PAUSE IN OUR PURSUIT
OF HAPPINESS AND
JUST BE HAPPY.

One universe,

9 planets,

204 countries,

809 islands,

7 seas . . .

and I had the

privilege

to meet you.

I THANK MY GOD
ALWAYS WHEN I REMEMBER
YOU IN MY PRAYERS.

· PHILEMON 1:4 ESV ·

At times our own light goes out and is rekindled by a spark from another person. Each of us has cause to think with deep gratitude of those who have lighted the flame within us.

(*Albert Schweitzer*)

Agree with
each other,
love each other, be
deep-spirited
friends.

PHILIPPIANS 2:2-3 MSG

DEAR LORD,

WHAT DID I DO TO DESERVE

SUCH GOODNESS? WHAT DID I

DO TO DESERVE SUCH BLESSING?

NOTHING! IT IS YOU WHO ARE

GOOD; IT IS YOU WHO BLESSED

ME WITH A GREAT FRIEND, AND I

THANK YOU WITH A FULL HEART.

HE WHO PLACED
THE STARS IN THE
HEAVENS
PLACED YOU IN
MY LIFE . . . AND
I AM TRULY
GRATEFUL.

To have a good friend is one of life's greatest delights; to be a good friend, one of the noblest undertakings.

—UNKNOWN

Let us love
one another: for
love is of God.

1 JOHN 4:7 KJV

Oh, the comfort,

THE INEXPRESSIBLE COMFORT

OF FEELING safe WITH A PERSON:

HAVING NEITHER TO

weigh thoughts nor

measure words,

BUT TO POUR THEM OUT.

JUST AS THEY ARE—

CHAFF *and* GRAIN TOGETHER,

KNOWING THAT A FAITHFUL HAND

WILL TAKE *and* SIFT THEM,

KEEP WHAT IS WORTH KEEPING,

and THEN WITH THE

breath of kindness,

BLOW THE REST AWAY.

George Eliot

It is in the SHELTER of each
other that people live.
—Irish proverb

Enter his gates with thanksgiving,
and his courts with praise!
Give thanks to him; bless his name!
For the Lord is good;
his steadfast love endures forever.

LOVE
adds
BEAUTY
to
LIFE.

IT IS NOT *joy*
THAT MAKES
US GRATEFUL. IT IS
GRATITUDE THAT
MAKES US *joyful*.

GRATITUDE . . .

GOES BEYOND THE "MINE" AND "THINE"
AND CLAIMS THE TRUTH THAT ALL OF
LIFE IS A PURE GIFT.
IN THE PAST I ALWAYS THOUGHT OF GRATITUDE
AS A SPONTANEOUS RESPONSE TO THE
AWARENESS OF GIFTS
RECEIVED, BUT NOW I REALIZE THAT

GRATITUDE CAN ALSO BE LIVED AS A DISCIPLINE. THE DISCIPLINE OF GRATITUDE IS THE EXPLICIT EFFORT TO ACKNOWLEDGE THAT ALL I AM AND HAVE IS GIVEN TO ME AS A GIFT OF LOVE, A GIFT TO BE CELEBRATED WITH JOY.

PHILLIP WARE, *HEARTLIGHT* MAGAZINE

Every time you cross my mind,
I break out in *exclamations*
of *thanks* to God.

—Philippians 1:3 MSG

AS WE GROW UP WE REALIZE
IT IS LESS IMPORTANT TO
HAVE LOTS OF FRIENDS

AND MORE IMPORTANT TO
HAVE REAL ONES.

THANK YOU
FOR BEING REAL.

While *love* is about mutual and binding affection, *esteem* is the high regard that comes with earning a place of respect in another's heart . . .

A Jane Austen Devotional

Not only do I love you,
I *esteem* you greatly.

LOVE FROM THE CENTER OF WHO YOU ARE . . . HOLD ON FOR DEAR LIFE TO GOOD.

—ROMANS 12:10 MSG

No
friendship
is an accident.

—O. HENRY

It may be true that
he travels farthest who
travels alone, but the
goal thus reached is
not worth reaching.

• THEODORE ROOSEVELT •

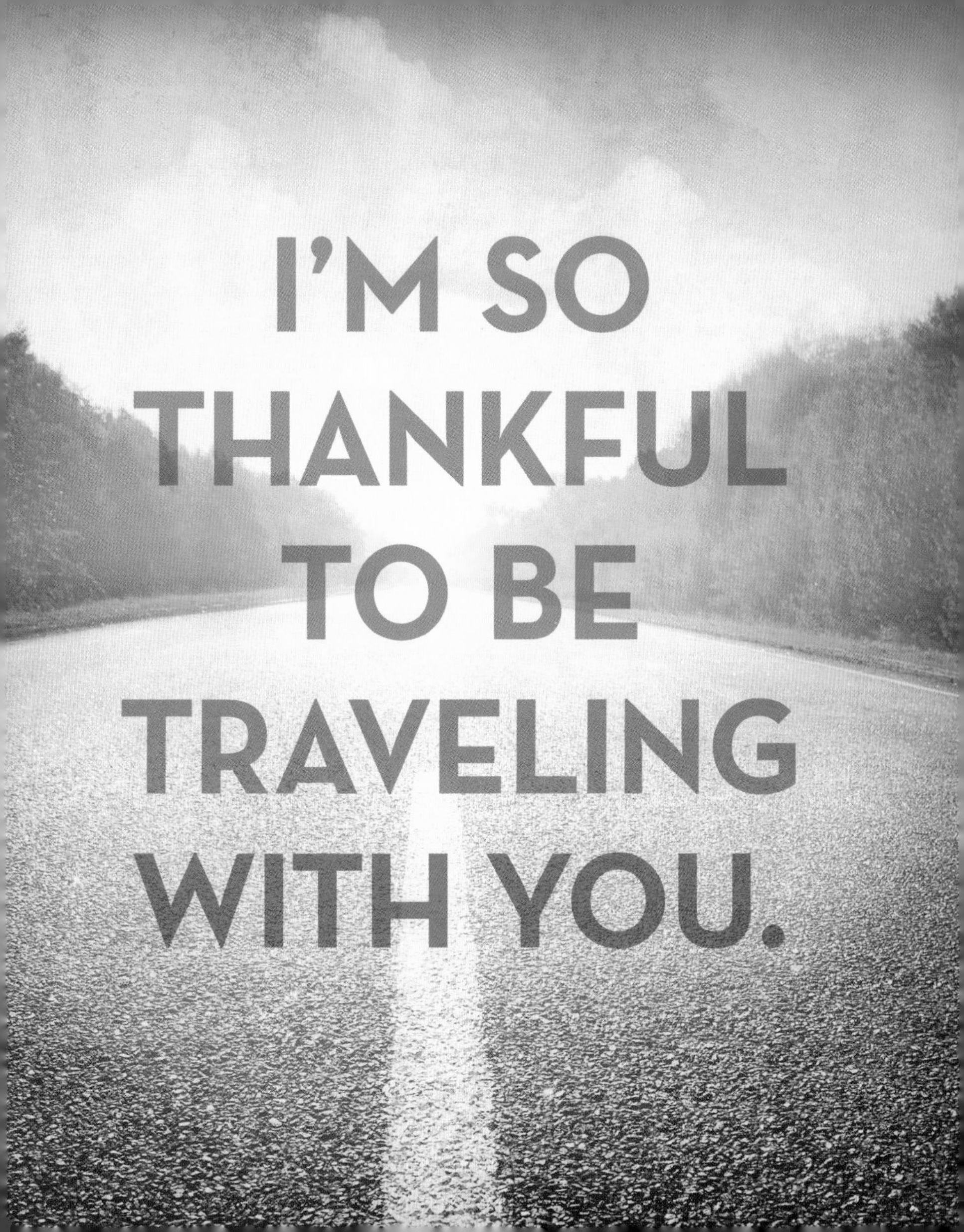

I'M SO THANKFUL TO BE TRAVELING WITH YOU.

THE HIGHEST
PRIVILEGE THERE IS,
IS THE PRIVILEGE
OF BEING ALLOWED
TO SHARE
ANOTHER'S LIFE.

YOU TALK ABOUT YOUR

pleasures

TO YOUR ACQUAINTANCES;

YOU TALK ABOUT YOUR

troubles

TO YOUR

friends.

Every good and perfect gift is from above.
—James 1:17

YOU ARE A
beautiful
GIFT *to* ME.

FRIENDSHIP ISN'T A BIG THING . . . IT'S A MILLION LITTLE THINGS.

How good you make others feel about themselves says a lot about you.

DEAR LORD, THANK YOU
FOR FRIENDS WHOSE *kindness*
SPILLS OVER INTO OTHERS' LIVES.
PLEASE HELP ME TO BE MORE LIKE
MY FRIEND— *loving, giving,*
thoughtful. A *humble*
REFLECTION OF YOU.

A
kind deed
performed
by a friend
is a *gift*
from *God.*

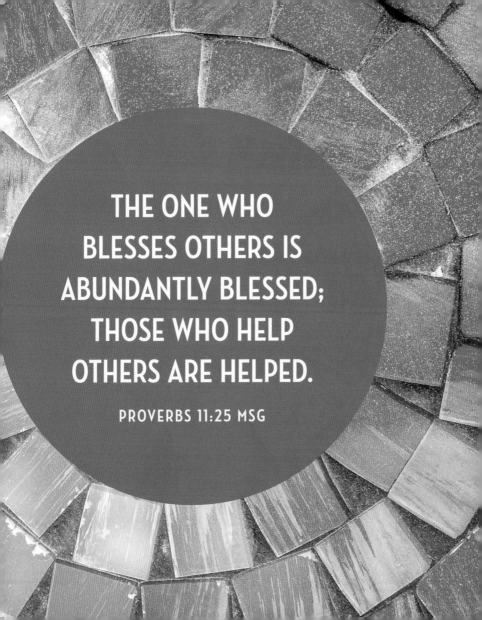

WE CAN FIND
OURSELVES IN THE
wilderness FROM
TIME TO TIME. THE
BIG *battle* COMES
IN TRUSTING THAT
GOD *will* PROVIDE
MANNA ENOUGH
FOR EACH *day.*

REAL FRIENDSHIP
IS SHOWN IN
TIMES OF TROUBLE;
PROSPERITY IS FULL
OF FRIENDS.

ABRAHAM KUYPER

True friendship is
a plant of slow growth,
and must undergo
and withstand the
shocks of adversity
before it is entitled
to the appellation.

George Washington

How perfectly this describes the way I feel about you:

"WITHOUT FRIENDS, NO ONE WOULD WANT TO LIVE, EVEN IF HE HAD ALL OTHER GOODS."

— Aristotle, The Nicomachean Ethics

HE FILLS MY LIFE WITH GOOD THINGS.

Psalm 103:5 NLT

I THANK HIM FOR YOU.

We give *thanks* to you, O God;

we give thanks, for your name is near.

We recount your *wondrous* deeds.

—PSALM 75:1 ESV

O Lord, what a privilege to live knowing that we are Your children! Thank You for seeing fit to save us and love us with an incomparable love, so that we might love one another.

FRIENDSHIP DOUBLES OUR JOYS AND HALVES OUR GRIEF.

A friend
IS SOMEONE
WHO KNOWS
THE *song* IN
YOUR *heart*
AND CAN *sing*
IT BACK TO YOU
WHEN YOU HAVE
forgotten
THE WORDS.

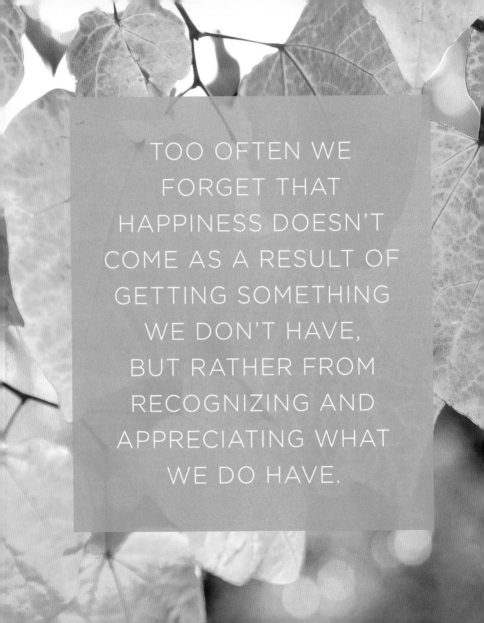

TOO OFTEN WE
FORGET THAT
HAPPINESS DOESN'T
COME AS A RESULT OF
GETTING SOMETHING
WE DON'T HAVE,
BUT RATHER FROM
RECOGNIZING AND
APPRECIATING WHAT
WE DO HAVE.

I'm
grateful
to have
you in
my life.

There is nothing
that makes us love
someone so much as
praying for them.

William Law

May you be richly rewarded by the LORD, the God of Israel, under whose wings you . . . take refuge.

RUTH 2:12

Value the least gifts no less than the greatest, and simple graces as special favors.

THOMAS À KEMPIS

Good friends are among
our greatest blessings—they
may keep us back from much
evil, quicken us in our course,
speak a word in season, draw
us upward, and draw us on.

J. C. Ryle

"I [CAN'T] STOP THANKING GOD FOR YOU—EVERY TIME I [PRAY], [I] THINK OF YOU AND GIVE THANKS. BUT I DO MORE THAN THANK. I ASK—ASK THE GOD OF OUR MASTER, JESUS CHRIST, THE GOD OF GLORY—TO MAKE YOU INTELLIGENT AND DISCERNING IN KNOWING HIM PERSONALLY, YOUR EYES FOCUSED AND CLEAR, SO THAT YOU can see exactly what it is he is CALLING you to do, grasp the IMMENSITY of this GLORIOUS way of LIFE he has for his followers, oh, the utter EXTRAVAGANCE of his work in us who trust him—endless ENERGY, boundless STRENGTH!"

Ephesians 1:15–19 msg

The
WORSHIP MOST
ACCEPTABLE *to*
GOD COMES FROM
a THANKFUL *and*
CHEERFUL HEART.

Plutarch

*Sing to the LORD with grateful praise;
make music to our God on the harp.*

—Psalm 147:7

How truly is a kind heart a
fountain of gladness, making
everything in its vicinity to
freshen into smiles.

WASHINGTON IRVING

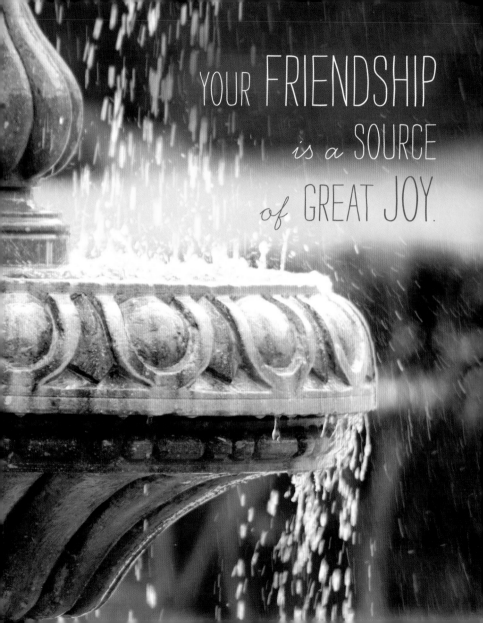

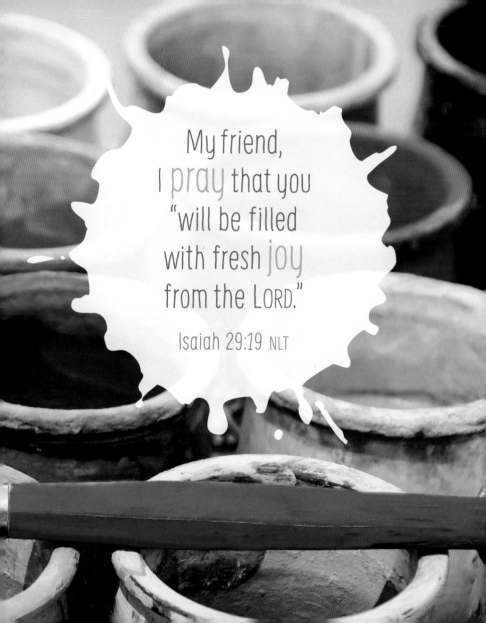

My friend,
I pray that you
"will be filled
with fresh joy
from the LORD."

Isaiah 29:19 NLT

Let us be grateful
to the people who
make us happy; they
are the charming
gardeners who make
our souls blossom.

—MARCEL PROUST

LET YOUR ROOTS GROW
DOWN INTO HIM, AND LET
YOUR LIVES BE BUILT ON HIM.
THEN YOUR FAITH WILL
GROW STRONG IN THE TRUTH
YOU WERE TAUGHT, AND
YOU WILL OVERFLOW WITH
THANKFULNESS.

COLOSSIANS 2:7 NLT

GRATITUDE IS HAPPINESS DOUBLED BY WONDER.

— G. K. CHESTERTON —

Kindred spirits
are not so scarce
as I used to think.
It's splendid to
find out there are
so many of them
in the world.

• L. M. MONTGOMERY, *ANNE OF GREEN GABLES* •

We give thanks to you, O God;
we give thanks, for your name is near.
We recount your wondrous deeds.

PSALM 75:1 ESV

ONE OF THE MOST
beautiful
QUALITIES OF TRUE
friendship
IS TO UNDERSTAND
AND TO BE UNDERSTOOD.

Lucius Annaeus Seneca

I'M SO GRATEFUL THAT ONE OF THE LIVES YOU'VE TOUCHED IS MINE.

GOOD FRIENDS
LAUGH, CRY, AND
ENCOURAGE EACH OTHER.
BUT MOST IMPORTANT,
TRUE FRIENDS POINT
ONE ANOTHER
TO JESUS.

I find myself
praying for you
with a glad
heart.

—Philippians 1:3 MSG

DEAR *heavenly* FATHER, THANK YOU FOR PLACING SOMEONE IN MY LIFE WHO POINTS ME TO YOU . . . WHO *spurs* ME TO LIVE

IN A WAY THAT PLEASES YOU. I *pray* THAT I CAN BE MORE LIKE THIS DEAR ONE IN IMITATING AND *glorifying* YOU.

TRUE FRIENDSHIP IS LIKE SOUND HEALTH: ITS VALUE IS SELDOM FULLY REALIZED UNTIL IT IS LOST.

There is *nothing* I would not do for those who are really my friends. I have no notion of *loving* people by halves, it is not my *nature*.

———

JANE AUSTEN, *Northanger Abbey*

Each time you come to
mind I think, *Thank You,
Lord, for such a dear friend.*

In everything
give thanks;
for this is
God's will
for you in
Christ Jesus.

1 THESSALONIANS 5:18 NASB

If you have a friend worth loving,

Love him. Yes, and let him know

That you love him, 'ere life's evening

Tinge his brow with sunset glow.

Why should good words ne'er be said

Of a friend—till he is dead?

ALEXANDER MACLEOD

ABOVE ALL, KEEP LOVING

ONE ANOTHER EARNESTLY,

SINCE LOVE COVERS A

MULTITUDE OF SINS. SHOW

HOSPITALITY.... AS EACH

HAS RECEIVED A GIFT, USE

IT TO SERVE ONE ANOTHER,

AS GOOD STEWARDS.

1 Peter 4:8–10 esv

HOLD A TRUE FRIEND WITH BOTH YOUR HANDS.

Nigerian proverb

If I had a *flower* for every time I thought of you . . . I could walk through my garden forever.

Alfred, Lord Tennyson

THANKFUL
I AM . . .
THAT YOU
ARE IN
MY LIFE.

Light
is sweet,
and it is
pleasant
for the eyes
to *see* the
sun.

ECCLESIASTES 11:7 ESV

You beam a lovely *brightness* into my heart.

Gratitude is the memory of the heart.

—JEAN MASSIEU

Cheerfulness
and *contentment* are
great beautifiers, and are famous
preservers of good looks.

—*Charles Dickens*

Mercy,
peace and
love be
yours in
abundance.

—JUDE 1:2

I PRAY GOD MULTIPLIES BACK TO YOU THE BLESSING YOU ARE MANY TIMES OVER.

the
BLESSING
of THE
LORD
BE ON YOU.

PSALM 129:8

May he give
you the desire of
your heart and make
all your plans succeed.

PSALM 20:4

I HAVE LEARNED
THAT TO BE
WITH THOSE I
LOVE IS ENOUGH.

Walt Whitman

May the LORD
continually bless you with
heaven's blessings as well
as with human joys.

PSALM 128:5 TLB